SCARS INTO GOLD

Healing Through the Power of Words —
From Trauma to Transformation

By Stella Magal

Conscious Dreams
PUBLISHING

Stars Into Gold: Healing Through the Power of Words —
From Trauma to Transformation

Copyright © 2025: Stella Magal

All rights reserved. No part of this publication may be produced, distributed, or transmitted in any form or by any means, including photocopying, recording, or other electronic or mechanical methods, without the prior written permission of the publisher, except in the case of brief quotations embodied in critical reviews and certain other non-commercial uses permitted by copyright law.

Published by Conscious Dreams Publishing
www.consciousdreamspublishing.com

Book Consultant: Daniella Blechner

Edited by Elise Ebram

Typeset by Oksana Kosovan

Cover Design by Emily's World of Design

Original Cover artwork by Stella Magal

ISBN: 978-1-917584-64-7

PREFACE

The title **Scars Into Gold** draws inspiration from Kintsugi, the Japanese art of repairing pottery with veins of gold. Known as the "golden repair," it is both a craft and a philosophy. One that finds beauty in imperfection and honours the history carried within every crack. In the same way, the human journey of healing transforms the ruptures of trauma into scars of strength, resilience and beauty.

I invite you into a space where scars are not only accepted but cherished as part of what makes us unique and whole. I release my poems from the personal to the collective with a wish that they take root in your life, transforming, evolving, and becoming uniquely meaningful to you.

The poems in this collection follow the cycles of grief within trauma. The grief for the parts of us that never received love. Love is our birthright, and when it goes unfulfilled, it elicits a deep sorrow … a pain that rises from the soul's unmet expectation.

In a world deeply starved of soul nourishment, I believe there is a vital and growing need for spaces of emotional truth, spiritual reflection, and deep connection. This book is my offering to that need.

DEDICATION

For Jane, who received my trembling voice like a prayer, mirroring back the light I could not yet see in myself. You held space for the first breath of this poetry and in doing so, began its becoming.

For Seraphina, tireless keeper of the flame, whose fierce love, deep faith, and unwavering presence have lit my path whenever I lost confidence. You have been the empowering doula to this book's birth.

For Avi, the great love of my life; 25 years of marriage, ever-evolving, ever creating beauty together. Thank you for being my roots and my rock, grounding me whenever I falter. I love you!

For every soul walking the path of healing, may you find your voice, your power, your peace.

CONTENTS

Threshold One — Archaeology of the Heart

Disassociation 12
Minimising 14
The Truth Teller 15
Battle Wastelands 17
Bringing Them Home 19
The Dig 21
Metal Meditation 23

Threshold Two — The Raging Protest

Belly Fire 26
Defiance Rap 27
I Claim Freedom 28
If You Try 30
Roar 31
Rudiments 33
Stella 35
Incantation 36
Fire Meditation 38

Threshold Three — Crying Over the Bones

Attachment 40
Two But Not Two 42
Wordless 43
Pneuma 44
Protection on Repeat 45
Activation 46
Suppression 47
Expectation v Reality 48
The Lost 49
Rip 50
Your Artist's Hand — For my brother Theni 51
Water Meditation 52

Threshold Four — The Sober Journey Home

Breaking Before Dawn 56
Bones 58
A Moment 59
The Melting 60
Little One 61
My Mother Nature 62
Honouring The Parts 64
Earth Meditation 65

Threshold Five — Integration's Embrace

Calling Back 68
Metamorphosis in Suspension 70
Jane 73
Absorb 74
Kali 76
Circles 78
Paradox Planet 80
The Crone Emerges 81
Rising Reclamation 83
The Passing 85
The Wheelbarrow Girl — A Soul Retrieval 86
Air Meditation 88

Acknowledgements 91
About the Author 93

Threshold One — Archaeology of the Heart

An excavation of the past. Using tools of curiosity and patience. With delicate care and precision, we explore what is waiting to be found within our hearts. This is the work of the seeking soul, feeling and listening for the scattered parts of us that long to be whole. Shock, freeze, denial, numbness: each one whispers through our dreams, *please, find me*.

Disassociation

Grey veils fall on jagged-edged thoughts. Layer upon layer: silk … cotton … velvet … canvas … each heavier than the next. A final weighted blanket buries the spiky lot, and the room fills with fog

dullness

and whipped confusion settles on a thick black coffee head

thoughts are slippery eels; their oily skins resist the grasp to know, and into a murky pool they go

whilst words become chalky letters, board dusted — blown away on hot breath

defeat and surrender merge in a dissonant dance

as I try to open clarity's door with a melting key

nothing can be voiced inside the anaconda's slow squeeze

I gasp for air and break the spell. Amnesia's army dispel. They run for the hills of my brow, out of sight behind the crest, waiting

waiting

for the next call

to save me.

Minimising

Soft, power persuasion, a song on repeat. Diminish, downplay, deny … diminish, downplay, deny. Hypnotising, mesmerising, shrinking the boulder of heavy truth, smaller and smaller into a pebble. Pushed deep into the meat of your bones, into the smallest chamber of your soul.

Sometime later. Minutes or centuries apart, the time will come when contraction cannot bear itself, when expansion chases itself together. When we are safe, when we are brave, synapses fire their neuronal knowing. A billion brain cells explode with electric truth. Oblivion is dead. And Goddess Alethia rises from our tongues.

The Truth Teller

Dandelions grow in unforgiving soil
as she did
breaking through
leaving behind her womb companion
saturated, waterlogged
to incarnate into magnetic mayhem
where Narcissus reigns intoxicated
unsatiable in his own demise

lies on repeat
are lullabies in an infant brain
voices and eyes cut
the fragments wrapped
each piece inside pretty clothes
posed

quietly she grows
cradling the pain
cuddling the shame
waiting for the day

the day when the secret submerged
the silent
the unnamed, the choked
can rise

the truth-teller will ignite the buried
light the dark
drag its stormy Neptune
into the dawn
tearing down his dusty rings
to illuminate his illusions
and when she's spoken all
she leaves

like a
dying
sun.

Battle Wastelands

Time bombs, flowing in veins
detonations of the unspeakable
buried in the bunkers of her brain
and memory fragments are
shards of pain
jolting, bolting electric.
Each morning, adrenaline rises
an acid fountain searing through flesh
and metal explodes, its spikes pierce heart and lungs
and all quantum spaces within.
Daily triggers hide in the unlikely
in the mundane
the smell of Chanel N°5
or rain on a windowpane.
And they sit on thin skin
agitating
waiting for the angry voice
the child's cry
the lover to leave
the marriage to end.
Trauma has taken her captive
the legacy locked her up
placed a guard named Shame
in a section of her brain

and a frozen frenzy, a trapped retaliation
in a buzzing body remains.
This body carries all
all day long, until it drops its weight
onto her pillow
attempting to be seen in her dreams
the scenes where her life was threatened
on repeat.
Murder rises from the neuron trenches
and she is neon wide awake whilst asleep.

Complex PTSD veterans of household wars
walk in the streets
invisible
and the bystanders blank behind the eyes
still stand by.

Bringing Them Home

Her name was spat from tight lips and empty eyes
with cold contempt
crushing her reach, demolishing her grasp
smashing her unfettered run
until she shattered
into a hundred particle pieces
diamonds embedded into floorboards
under snatched rugs and beneath feet
sending prisms of light
to the centre of the earth
where her battered heart
hid

there was a place
warrior guarded, waiting
for the safe day
where she could recoup and speak her truth
when her longing for the lost
broke free
and the painful, sweet search
began

she gathered the fragments
the terrified, shaking veins
the horrified, frozen limbs
the secrets embedded in bones
the bits and pieces of amorphous pain
the exiled parts of her that had to run
she brought them all home
one by one
until a million carats of light
shone from her eyes.

The Dig

History's inflictions held in bones
calcium memories fossilised
and found within
it's what we do in circles of women
our hands are tools for the dig
the unforgotten, under our fingernails

as the moon turns in our bodies
her cycles shed layers
revealing untruths
we women are Way Finders
we are the litmus test
our bodies barometers of knowing
we **feel** the lies as we weep them out

in the end, life will erode all that we hold
all we control
clenched fists ache with a will to let go

so, let's first cry ourselves alive
and rise from the rubble, the wreckage
of so-called civilised life
let's remove arrow tips
from each other's flesh

by first feeling our own wounds
and wording them whole
as spirit and soul knit
knits them together
and we'll feel our pain fall
like ripe fruit from its branch

women in circles — witnessing, excavating
with kindness, always kindness
kindness will be my balm
and at sorrow's pace, I'll mend
that which is found fractured, all that's found
just as fast as nature's slowest
healing in rock time
nature holding my impatient hand
as we dig the archaeology of the heart.

Metal Meditation

As we've journeyed through the Archaeology of the Heart threshold, the metal meditation helps us to connect with the inherent strength we have within, that we don't always feel. It reminds us of how taking the first brave steps will lead to something precious. Something golden.

- Find a metal object that's special to you or provides some comfort.
- Speak to it — saying, 'I ask that your energy of conductivity and solidness supports my connection with my heart.'
- Find a comfortable place to sit or lie down.
- Observe your natural breath for a minute.
- Tune in to the energy of metal: connection, strength, courage, stability, balance and purification.
- Breath these energies into your body to any areas that feel depleted or in pain.
- Bring compassion and acceptance to whatever rises.
- The metal element helps reduce stress, purifies the body, and enhances intuition and emotional well-being.

Threshold Two — The Raging Protest

Anger — the natural emotion that had to be suppressed in order to survive. It is now essential for this protective energy to be ignited. For individuation, growth of thwarted parts of self to flourish in its passion and for healthy boundaries against threat or injustice to be created.

Belly Fire

So sure of myself
wild horses or green-eyed mothers
can't stop me now!
I shall write the buried wrath-free
the words rumble
thunderclaps shake awake my fingertips
as pecking birds on the keyboard
wing their way to open windows
wild freedom
expressing the repressed

not so sure of myself
as doubt seeps into the day's retreat
and dusk settles in defeat

but I feel the embers
smoldering in my womb
I am Creatrix, howling at the moon
tonight, I am more wolf than woman!

I call in the 'Begin Again'
the transforming turns to snake
rubbing off her skin

rebirth isn't pretty.

Defiance Rap

You tried to hurt and destroy me
But that will never be
I don't fear you because I'm free
Your armour is your demise
I will rise
I am not your projections
They do not harbour in me
They are just reflections
Your words are not my belief
I transform at the core, a relief
You are not the fantasy I created
It was an illusion, it was fake
All you ever did was take
Superficial, small crumbs of kindness
Tiny glimpses of hope, just blindness
As you destroy love, you create chaos
You annihilate intimacy and trust
I tried to pour love on your coldness
But ended up frozen and useless
As I try to escape, you lure back and entice
Then, controlling anger strangles and rage bites
Storms of confusion
Finally over, your words erroneous
Eclipsed
The End.

I Claim Freedom

I was lost
coiled inside a stone
now I'm unfurling, revealing
undeniably appearing

how do I begin to be me
with you?
when I rise, you crush me
I am of no use to you
unless I'm holding you up

love and compassion fail to thrive
when under siege

you look puzzled, as I speak
do I not behave as I once did?
is this change, this liberation, a conundrum?
the unnamed pain
always rises from its hiding
surfacing from the dark ocean bed
the chains have worn through
and gravity is law

I shine a light on the ghosts
those who once wronged me
they wish to atone for their vented venom
once poured on my childhood dreams
they beg forgiveness
I commence reparation's repair
and lay them to rest
just dead people now
their shadows will not lurk
in the corners of my life
and no longer will their legacy
harbour in me.

If You Try

… to take the wind out of my sails, I will kick up a storm. I will Be the wind.

If you try to fearmonger, I will shoot to the margins of that fear and grow the space. I will Be expansion.

If you try to disable me with your cynicism, I will explode into optimism. I will Be a supernova.

If you are the killjoy to my dreams, I will call the biggest party to my door. I will be the loudest, most colourful carnival you've ever seen! I will Be joy.

I warn you now: don't try to take me down. It's futile. Your darkness is the catalyst for my light. Sunrise would be nothing without the dark moon night. So maybe we'll just be who we are, two sides of the same coin.

When you try, I will grow. This is how I roll.

Roar

Your voice long dead
still echoes, reverberates in my head
your arrowed words
pierced
your hand rained down on my innocence
stinging humiliation
systematic breaking
no one came to my rescue
no safety
no recourse but to return
to enmesh with the enemy

'mummy' should conjure memories of kindness and care
instead, a trap holding me in its lair
the hand that should caress
was a weapon at every stress
the words that should soothe
were arsenals of war at every move
ricochet with contempt
defenceless, never exempt
from your tests, I failed
to anticipate your rage
assailed
battle worn

left forlorn
self-esteem torn

a phoenix, I will rise!
struggling to revive
a life without pain
my aim
to mourn
to transform
to be, for me, for all … seen or obtuse
survivors of abuse.

Rudiments

A plethora of potential in petrified stone, fossilised frozen life. Flourishing hammered, actualisation squashed. Every call from within stifled, every shoot reaching for the sunlight returned to the dark earth. It was lethal to grow, so sovereignty waited in another realm. Safety said, 'Stay small, smaller than small, tiny and deathly still.'

In the stillness, I transformed into water. Fluid. Unbreakable. Flowing through the double binds. 'Don't be happy, don't be sad, don't be wild, don't be tame, don't be energetic, don't be slow, don't be expressive, don't be pensive, don't be quiet, don't be loud. Stop reading, stop playing, stop laughing, stop crying, stop singing, stop studying, stop running, stop sleeping. Don't do handstands, don't do cartwheels, don't paint, don't ask, don't sink feet into sand, don't jump puddles. Don't write poetry. Don't exist.'

These voices, these echoes from my mother's, grandmother's, great-grandmother's mouths … thundering backwards and forwards through ether to the ancestors, to the zero point, the causal, where the violence began! Back and back to the inception, to the first dark act.

Trauma ceaselessly runs from itself. Racing inexhaustible, through generation upon generation. Healthy bulbs trodden down within icy ground. Saplings crushed every spring. Buds severed every summer. Leaving decimated, desecrated topsoil.

But I never stopped hearing the husks breaking.

I never stopped feeding the seeds with my dreams.

I never stopped.

Stella

I call you to the bone
I call you to the flesh
so we can feel the breath
of
each other …

Incantation

I wrote a prayer for you, Mum
I wish it was full of love
I wish it brimmed with gratitude
I wish I could say your name, without pain

I wrote a prayer for you, Mum, a eulogy to lost hope
I wish your words had cradled my childish joy
and that your smile had flooded light into dark nights
I wish your hands were soft on my baby skin
and your eyes had seen heaven in me

I wish your hands hadn't reigned terror in my flesh
I wish your words hadn't been bullets in my heart
I wish your actions weren't poison in my brain

The torment curled into my cells

I wish the horror would say goodbye, just implode
to leave behind a void, a black hole
a place to howl the unspeakable
a place to hold the unholdable

I implore the Karma Masters
I beseech the Time Lords to unravel time
how would this matter? Please
bring me a different kind of mum, a kind mum

May my words be
a good spell
to change the past
to erase it and replace it
with a mum who was healed and well.

Fire Meditation

Our bodies are made up of all the elements and here we are connecting with the spirit of fire. This connection evokes the power that is needed for transformation and transmutation. Fire energy is passion and sacred anger, both essential ingredients for the healing process.

- I invite you to light a fire or light a candle in a safe, inside space.
- Notice how your body feels as you make yourself cosy and comfortable.
- Become aware of your breath, and take a few gentle, deeper breaths.
- Gently gaze at the fire/candle as you inhale, and release tension as you exhale. Imagine every hurt and injustice dissolving, carried away and embraced by the benevolent energy of fire.
- Ask the fire 'please transmute and purify all that doesn't serve me'.
- Surrender all your pain to Grandfather Fire. Ask for truth to be illuminated within your heart. Gently ask what wants to be revealed to you.
- The fire element will energise, purify, illuminate and enlighten.

Threshold Three — Crying Over the Bones

Grief, pain and sorrow for all that was lost and endured. Sacred tears. Surrender, surrender, surrender to the mighty flow.

Attachment

Always just out of sight
like changing chameleon colours
where the interface of cactus green
slips away

into desert grey

morphing into a mirage
where fingers fail to grasp
left lost
longing and empty

safety obliterated
incinerated in the furnace
of trauma

until she dares to feel
the scorched deserted parts within
and takes their pain to the threshold
to the altar
of lost connections …

connections lost …

connections …

connections …

Two But Not Two

I knew of death before I knew of life
I knew death was life
I knew life was death
indivisible
you taught me that

As inseparable as sunrise and sunset
as bound as stars in the night sky
we remained
my grasp for you, embedded in my fingers
you gave me that
my stillborn twin

You returned to eternal life
to oneness with the divine
within every tiny cell
and in the universe
you exist

As the moon resides in the heavens
and in the night lake's face
we will always be both two and one
you told me that

and then you left.

Wordless

I see you through the stifled pain

your ears heard the sounds
from their lips, their puzzled frowns
looking at an alien, only three foot high
brown skin, brown eyes

their voices made similar sounds
'What's wrong?' I hear you say
'Then katalavéno.' 'I don't understand'

lost and landed on a hostile plain
in a white middle-class
classroom
I was the little Greek girl
with no words
and a strange name.

Pneuma

Melded
molded
climbed into a sarcophagus
into a lost soul limbo

the tomb's inscription
rises from history's ashes
a gold epitaph reads
'The Deathless One'

its single
erratic pulse
senses my breath
my heart wills its beat
and I plead, and I roar

Rise. Rise. Rise!

Protection on Repeat

You have survived
but you keep running to find safety
unaware that you have already
found it.

Activation

Disillusionment falls like heavy bricks, burying me in my bed. Attunement blocked by mortar, and all is dead.

Suppression

Words
are frosty knots in my throat
unable to unravel down my tongue.

Thoughts chase them back to
the spongy cavern in my head
where they lay on frozen beds.

Expectation v Reality

An unsatisfactory, ethereal relationship.
Do they ever meet each other's needs?
Conflict and disappointment
interlaced with creamy hope.

The Lost

A cloud of grey sorrow moves over the sun. A dull hammering in a distant place
draws me closer, into the wilderness. Revealing its sound as the repeated knocking of nails into the coffin where my five-year-old exuberance lies.

Rip

Nails itching to pick and peel
at curling corners

it was Mum's mad choice, the Taj Mahal gold, slapped on adjacent walls, to Dad's flower-embossed rebellion. Sitting like a sick joke. Pasted on touching edges.

Edges, blade sharp.

Your Artist's Hand —
For my brother Theni

Your hands. Brown —
    Caressing infant memories
Your hands. Red —
    Painting embers in a child's mind
Your hands. Yellow —
    Holding nicotine tubes and bubble wands
Your hands. White —
    Swollen, cancer-worn
Your hands. Violet —
    Touching angels' wings.

Water Meditation

Water is considered sacred in many cultures around the world. Much of Earth's surface is covered in water so it teaches us about the interconnectivity of all life and particularly to our own bodies that are made up of 60% water.

- Water soothes, supports and facilitates flow of emotions.
- I invite you to sit or lie on the floor, making yourself cosy and comfortable where you won't be disturbed. Or perhaps find a quiet place in nature.
- Fill a bowl or vessel with water. As you do, speak words of kindness, love and compassion into it. Connect with its mutable, unbounded energy.
- Take three deeper breaths, releasing tension on your exhale. Enquire into what most needs to be released — memories, thoughts, emotions, physical tension — in the body and exhale it into the water.

- Ask the water's wisdom to absorb and transmute what isn't needed anymore.
- The water element brings flexibility, flow and unbounded love. Allow any tears to flow. Welcome and honour them. They too are sacred.
- Finally, pour the water into Mother Earth or a place in nature. Ask for her unconditional love to transmute and alchemise all that's been released and to use it for her nourishment.
- Give gratitude for yourself and sacred water that supports you.

Threshold Four — The Sober Journey Home

The solemn acceptance of truth. The bright light of authenticity that no longer wants to hide behind distractions and numbing. No more running from the self. Grief has carried us into our true selves before the damage was done. We arrive back to nature. Back into our earthy bodies. We expand our capacity to feel our pain, to embrace the many parts of ourselves and to bring them into the light of awareness.

Breaking Before Dawn

Parts push into chaos, like funfair dodgems colliding, metal on metal, 'it's a storm in a headcup'. Retaliation and shame throw its icy pellets against the windowpane.
    It's a perfect storm.

Protectors swoop down from black clouds to rescue the drowning, and just as I feel the panic, there it comes, the
    Might Relief of disassociated sleep,
              sinking,
              sinking into a pink mousse
              bed — further still to La La Land
              oblivion.

But peace is a far-off land.

Icy water crashes into warm flesh and a sleepy head.
A jolted mind says, 'Things to do, people to see, places to go go go!'

Enters the Night Watchman, whose shift never ends, setting off the alarm, yelling into synapses, 'How can you sleep? The house is on fire! Danger, infiltrating you're offline! Remember the imposters who ransacked the sacred and burnt you alive.' Electric blood runs me wide awake!!!

       into a swarm of bees and the bees become
       meS. What a disguise — a cavalry

       in black and yellow stripes — flit, flit, hover
       fly — each flower's sweet nectar better than
       the next — sending me

   hither and thither.

I peel myself from the sheets

and into sobering morning light.

Feet on cold floor, shame
descending a concrete cape draped
     on my back.

     I catch the mirror's reflection … a chalky pallor of
     overwhelm covers my skin.

Oh, I pray for the sunshine of my true self to shine on the
storm-broken parts of me.
    To clear the dark disorder and
    let Love take them all into its ever-present embrace.

Bones

I've started sleeping with a soft blanket held to my cheek. This strange calling rose from my blood, repeating its request until I acquiesced. Infant demands unmet stay still inside the flesh and cries nestled in old bones crescendo to the skin. Yearning tactile on fingertips.

My hands caress the blanket's smooth breast. I am full of milky softness.

Time rewritten.

A Moment

I've come to love rainy, grey days. They patter and cry down windowpanes. 'Look how we contrast with the bright, golden sun. Our chalky drizzle is a prelude, a curtain-raiser. Without us, blue sky days fall into banality; no gratitude will come their way. We are the place of watery peace stillness. Part of the majestic whole.'

The Melting

I shall lay down my fear, not with malice or disdain but with grace. I shall lay it down … release, as if lowering a leaf on a flowing river … tenderly … my attachment to its familiar grip, the one that's ready to fight, this, too … I'll let it drip from my fist. I shall kick off my tight shoes that stifle my growth, their scuffs are warrior wounds. I shall let mistrust unfurl from the womb of my cells … the ancestral pain uncoil from my DNA, melt away in the fire of my belly … and an aperture will grow in the avenues and vistas of my flesh and bones where terror once lived, ready to receive the light that's flooding in.

Little One

Welcome
I shall let you curl in my womb
squeeze you, flesh to flesh
as we
the me of the past and now
shall grow in muffled waters
lapping heavily with love
where … slow … is … best

safe
until all the stars burn out
and even then
yes … even then.

My Mother Nature

We played in the woods, running from tree to tree, dappling sunlight touching our tousled hair and flickering kaleidoscopes on our skin. I still remember that musty, earthy smell and the spongy moss at my feet. I hear our echoed voices in the hollowed tree where we sat dreaming our dreams … the non-ordinary world became our norm … wood spirits, fairies, and wise owls, teaching us their lessons of presence, connection, and Oneness. Every tree had its own special magic. We named them 'The Elephant', 'The Old Man', 'The Castle'. The ancient ones came alive with our stories. Deeper and deeper into the lower earth's wonders we'd go. Dragons and Merlins, snowy diamond-peaked mountains, home-built rafts on stormy seas and silver rockets to the stars.

Reluctantly, returning to our sober homes each night … and without fail, they'd welcome us back come rain or shine, a haven on scorching blue-sky days or a canopy from sudden storms. We slipped into this realm with ease; the door was always open for us. It was our Sanctuary. We'd run inside, falling on our backs, laughing, panting steamy breaths, and flaying our sweaty limbs in the air. Earth and sky meeting inside our little bodies.

The alchemy of those blessed days remains with me today, nestled in my maturity, in my ripe memories.

Oh, what fortune, to be wild children … running in the woods. Tasting carefreeness and being loved … by the True Mother.

Honouring The Parts

Little one, who are you? Camouflaged in pain. Inside a spring in my jaw and curled in my chest. I'm ready to know you

to hold you … can you step out of the shadows into the light? The light that will flood into all of our dark rooms if we open the doors, just a chink. You can never displease me. Unconditionally, I embrace you … wholeheartedly, I feel you … ready

to know what chased you into those secret chambers. I am strong and able to know your truth. I can bear witness to the burdens and the unburdening and I bow in honour of your release. I shall kiss your feet.

Who protects you? Can I know you, too? I whisper a silk touch promise of eternal love.

Little one and your Protectors: The Critic, The Manager, The Energy Sapper, The Dreamer, The Runner, The Pleaser … you are all a sacred part of me … what tireless roles you've endlessly played to help me survive. Now I invite you to play in innocence, in awe, in wonder, in adventure and in magic … by the fires, in the waters, in the air and on the earth. Little one and all — I have arrived at the Cave of Lost Souls … to the little children who wait … I am coming.

Earth Meditation

Earth is our mother. She is a living breathing being that provides all for us unconditionally. Enter this deep honouring of her as she supports your healing. Mother Earth receives us with her enduring love and provision.

- I invite you to take some deep, belly breaths, releasing any tension that's built up in your body.
- Either sitting or lying down, visualise golden roots from your base growing deep into the earth.
- Imagine those roots wrapping around a rock deep in the centre of Mother Earth, holding you safe and secure.
- Visualise a space in nature that is protected and safe and just for you. Allow the earth's energies of security, abundance, unconditional love, balance and trust to flow into your body. Breath these energies into your heart space.
- The earth brings nourishment, nurturing, replenishment and balance.

Threshold Five — Integration's Embrace

Exiled parts of self coming together into wholeness;
bringing a deep sense of peace and freedom.
All the diamond facets shine together.
Honed in the troubled times.

Calling Back

Today, I found you in the misty hallways of a lost childhood
many years, I've searched in all the wrong places
to fill that hollow gut
longing

Today, I found you through fading fog
and I took your hand
showing you how far we've come
in all those years

I took you to the sea, which once shook
the memory of you … in me
and there we saw a sword, slicing the horizon
a sublime silver light that married sky with sea

Today, through the shadows
and out of the cave of my unconscious, you appeared
asking, 'Do you want me?'
your small, brave voice cracked my heart … open

Today, I found you
the veils fell away from my eyes
and the wind carried them afar
whilst the wild sea washed away the pain

And for the very first time
we exhaled together
a salty breath relief

she and me.

Metamorphosis in Suspension

Shapeless and unformed
she crawled into a cave
into a cave of lost souls
this little part of
me

I took this cave into my womb
as we walked our silent walk
year upon year, its wait ached
and her voice from within
echoed through my dreams

one safe day, I sensed
a single, erratic pulse
from this amorphous child
the pain of my stifled growth
oozed through my blood

and I felt her, and I felt her again
each breath blew oxygen into cells
and plumped her umbilical cord
I hugged her into my basal folds
and I felt her, and I felt her again

she started to whisper
in the gaps between my words
until her voice turned into vision
of her tiny foetal form … thwarted
and I felt her, and I felt her again

and when the safe days were plentiful
and ready to harvest
I felt her until I was full of her
grief flooded from DNA to skin
for the lost years … irreclaimable

only Nature's Doula could help
knowing the ancient ways
I felt the love of the trees and the mycelium
and the leaf-dappled sunbeams
where earth thawed

a carrion crow cawed
black rattling
a cycle's end
beckoning a beginning
and I felt her, and I felt her again

as she stretched and turned
and began to form in the waters
of my body
and I roared
thrive, thrive, thrive!

Jane

I don't know you in the common sense, in the periphery, in the chit-chat details.
I don't know you, no matter how I yearn to

I don't know whether sleep evades you after hearing and holding and bearing all the pain carried in and left heavy in your therapy room … in your Womb Room Temple

I don't know whether the crystals and the incense helped to lighten your vast heart, but each time I leave, I pray that they do

I don't know you in the common sense, but I know your essence and your truth. And I know not to know you, in your presence and in the absence, in that space,
I find the lost me.

Absorb

Let love seep into the fabric of your body and soul
and   let   love   flow
in plasma, in membranes, in your blood
into spaces imperceivable to the eye but vast to the heart

Let love imbue and surround each cell, muscle, bone and fibre
and let love be in each point
pulsing

Let love be your ears
so you hear the wordless within, the sublime speaking silence
so you hear what's shy behind your words

Let love be your voice so your spoken is true
let its caress be a salve on sore skin
and its resonance a mantra

Let love be your eyes so that sight awe inspires
and takes breath away
so the beauty you behold is received into your flesh

Feel love in the breeze, in the sea and the sun and the earth
let all your senses combine and immerse into the Oneness
that you are

Let love be in you, and you in it
until you know
to the marrow
to the core
THAT YOU ARE LOVE.

Kali

And there it was, the golden path
previously a sherbet mirage at every step
but today, I awoke blinded by its light
and there She was, Magnificent
risen from the depths of my flesh

Her roar vibrated in all of my being
shaking the prison doors that held me trapped
her voice penetrating, opening the wood's grain
chinks of sunlight flooded through
what was once solid

Stepping through the now hollow frame
the ancestral burdens, their weight
fell together with me
to the earth
to the Goddess's feet

She lifted me and carried me
to the dark womb
where I yielded, melting
in her fiery breath, dissolving
into her fierce love

I alchemised
pain to gold
as she breathed me in and out, and

back to life.

Circles

WOMEN, circle of fire!
Flesh and blood arisen from Gaia!
You are here standing and held
your heartbeats are drums in rhythm
with ALL of life!

You are imbued, filled to the brim
from your skin to your bones
with the power of the universe
your — bodies — are
volcanos, tsunamis
galaxies, primordial waters
meadows, multiverses
stars, silk and granite
you are the embodied Divine

It is your time
the power over paradigm
eclipsed the yin
in man and woman
let us awaken, reclaim *Shakti*
remember that which was dimmed

You are capable of so much more
than you've ever known
and now is the time to KNOW
a crystalline light has called you here
into circles of purity
sacred circles once denied
have returned … you have reclaimed them
raw and wild from your wombs to our wands

This is Your time
This is Your time
This is Your time

Time to Rise!

Paradox Planet

Consciousness, wanting to know itself
sparks the Divine
in the Dark Womb
and the Goddess gives birth
to duality

the dance of opposites begins:

where diving into darkness
becomes light exalted

where the more we cling
the further we push

where surrender allows us to heal
and vulnerability brings strength

where compassion blossoms from pain
and our wounds form shadows
so they can be seen

duality rests in the arms of paradox
and as our consciousness expands
we see the dance of contrast
as the Oneness of love.

The Crone Emerges

And so, it finally came
the day to be seen in my fullness
in my real rawness
and now I stand in the spotlight, quivering
holding the hand of a banished part of myself
once hidden in my heart
she wants to run for shelter
her protector descends from the wings of the stage
to the rescue
yelling into her flushed face, 'This Is Not Safe!
Who do you think you are, little caterpillar?
Stop now before you drown in mortification!'

I find myself off-stage in the wings
every fibre of my body seeks to hide in the scenery
merge with the stagehand
my past says, 'It's so much easier helping others to shine
holding them up and crouching in their shadow.'

Can I risk the audience's eyes
their stare, their gaze, their potential scorn?
and then my Cronehood volition broke the chrysalis open
it cracked the cramped, restrictive home
and emerged wet-winged, crinkled and gluey

am I ready to fly
can I step out of the stage wings
and let my wings dry in the spotlight sun?

Yes, I can see my fledgling flight
ascending in the springtime wind
and almost feel the rushing breeze
of a soaring ascent
on my shy skin.

Rising Reclamation

I am not pink
at least not candy floss
but ferocious fuchsia
tricking the eye with sunset's loss

I am not blue
not easel tube spread
dripping no matter what you do
but azure coral sea blue — sometimes shark black

I am not green
bowling grass green
unnaturally perfected and inspected
I am the wild green of the rain-rejoicing Amazon

I am not red
the stop light
I am unashamed menstrual red
vibrant flowing knowing

I am not amber
fossilised and extracted
I am the She Wolf rising
flashing ice amber eyes through nebulous dreams

I am not rainbows or orderly conformities
I am spectrums that shift and slide
and refuse to be confined
I am the light of the soul

The box your fear wrapped me
packed me into and comfortably labelled
only needs the smallest chink
for my escape.

The Passing

She died an unusual death. There were no shocks. No dreadful diagnoses. No furrow-browed family gathering to offer support. No treatment plans. No striving to survive.

It wasn't a sudden death or even a slow one. It was an imperceivable one. Except perhaps to those sensitive souls who feel the ending of things in deep and silent little omens. Black crows … single magpies … the burst of life soon to cease from the late summer blossom.

Each morning brought a little death. She left layers of herself in the dreamtime sheets. The days involved dissolution of her neat, defined identities and a crumbling of her hollowed-out certainties. The dying felt both painful and sweet.

One dark moon night, she softly stepped, like a surefooted black cat, over a threshold. The sort that didn't allow you back.

Echoes of her past resounded … all that was lay shrivelled like peeled snakeskin at her feet. She looked back at her LifeDeath and smiled. Because now she knew that in order to live fully, you have to die regularly.

The Wheelbarrow Girl — A Soul Retrieval

Over rocky terrain, her wheels bounce and roll
worn to the spoke on paths of endurance
I saw her appear in her grandmother's dreams
and in the shadowy psyche
rising up through the Shamanic drum

a little six-year-old, keeps walking towards the light
towards the beacon on the Himalayan peak
towards the singing of her tribe
towards her soul family's lullabies and lilts
she followed their homecoming songs
each sunrise a celebration of hope
each dark moon rekindled her courage
to see the next full moon
cycles of wheels and time became one

her wheelbarrow piled high with stories
books stacked, tumbling and weather-worn
her words preserved in glowing holograms
the whole present in each part

a little six-year-old kept walking
towards the light of the day
where ears and hearts could receive
where she could speak her travel-worn words
and poems would flow from her lips.

Air Meditation

Air symbolises the bird's eye view. Seeing the whole picture. The landscape of life's abrasions viewed from above, becomes a unified tapestry. All parts woven together.

- I invite you to find a pleasant place in nature. Perhaps up on a hill or a room with a door or window open.
- Set an intention … make it present tense, such as 'I am peace', 'I am worthy', 'I am whole'. 'My body is relaxed', Or anything that feels authentic for you.
- Breathe in for a count of six hold for two and exhale for eight or any rhythm that works better for you; just try to exhale for longer than your inhale. Focus on your breath.
- When you feel able to, become an observer. Become a witness to yourself.
- Begin to notice any sensations, thoughts, emotions or beliefs that might arise.

- You are held and safe in the breath of life, in Spirit. Stay with whatever arises with love.
- The air will bring clarity, a bird's eye view, the peaceful warrior energy and inspiration.
- Exhale all that doesn't serve you.
- Inhale the intention you set at the beginning.
- Each breath is a new birth.

ACKNOWLEDGEMENTS

My heartfelt gratitude goes to all whose talent, care, and dedication helped me birth this book.

To Danni, my publisher at Conscious Dreams Publishing (CDP), thank you for your belief in me. You understood my vision and were always aligned with my progress, encouraging me and keeping me on track throughout the whole process … always with kindness.

To Elise, whose edits were carried out with such respect and appreciation for my work, thank you for understanding my voice.

To Emily, my designer, thank you for so beautifully and skilfully incorporating my painting on the front cover.

To Jae, whose design skills brought my spiral paintings onto the threshold pages, and to Ces for her gold frames.

To my typesetter, Oksana, who put this book together and brought my vision to life.

To all of you behind the scenes at CDP, I appreciate you.

To my daughter, Zoe. Thank you for capturing me with such love and honesty in the photographs used for the back cover and other promotions, and for offering your professional graphic design reflections on my final stage choices. You always encourage me to stay true to myself.

To my daughter, Hannah, who always meets my poems with such admiration and love.

And to everyone who has walked beside me, thank you. Your presence, in all its forms, has helped voice the frequency held within these pages.

And to you, dear readers … thank you for walking this path beside me. I honour you.

ABOUT THE AUTHOR

Stella Magal is a poet whose work is rooted in personal healing from childhood trauma and spiritual connection. Her poetry weaves powerful metaphor, musicality, and profound insights into the human experience. She seamlessly merges the physical and the spiritual, crafting a unique voice that speaks to both mind and heart. Her vivid language invites readers to see the world anew, stirring the soul with authenticity and power.

A former social worker and psychodynamic therapist, Stella is also a trained shamanic practitioner. She creates channelled poems in healing sessions and performs at live events. Her creative process is nourished by nature, meditation, and yoga, and she believes poetry is vital soul nourishment in a world hungry for truth, healing, and authentic connection.

A devoted mother and grandmother, she shares a deep, living connection with her family, whom she describes as the heart of an ever-growing, unconditional love.

Conscious Dreams
PUBLISHING

Transforming diverse writers
into successful published authors

www.consciousdreamspublishing.com

authors@consciousdreamspublishing.com

Let's connect

www.ingramcontent.com/pod-product-compliance
Lightning Source LLC
Chambersburg PA
CBHW061223070526
44584CB00029B/3965